soy

soy

Great recipe ideas with a classic ingredient

>> in **60** ways

mc Marshall Cavendish
Cuisine

The publisher wishes to thank **Lim's Arts and Living** for the loan and use of their tableware.

Editor: Yong Kim Siang
Designer: Lock Hong Liang
Photographer: Joshua Tan, Elements by the Box

Published by Marshall Cavendish Cuisine
An imprint of Marshall Cavendish International
1 New Industrial Road, Singapore 536196

Other Marshall Cavendish Offices:
Marshall Cavendish Ltd. 119 Wardour Street, London W1F 0UW, UK • Marshall Cavendish Corporation. 99 White Plains Road, Tarrytown NY 10591-9001, USA • Marshall Cavendish International (Thailand) Co Ltd. 253 Asoke, 12 Flr, Sukhumvit 21 Road, Klongtoey Nua, Wattana, Bangkok 10110, Thailand • Marshall Cavendish (Malaysia) Sdn Bhd, Times Subang, Lot 46, Subang Hi-Tech Industrial Park, Batu Tiga, 40000 Shah Alam, Selangor Darul Ehsan, Malaysia

Marshall Cavendish is a trademark of Times Publishing Limited

National Library Board Singapore Cataloguing in Publication Data

Soy in 60 ways :- great recipe ideas with a classic ingredient. – Singapore :- Marshall Cavendish Cuisine,- c2007.
p. cm. – (In 60 ways)
ISBN-13 : 978-981-261-356-1
ISBN-10 : 981-261-356-0

1. Cookery (Soybeans) I. Title: Soy in sixty ways II. Series: In 60 ways

TX803.S6
641.65655 -- dc22   SLS2007015890

Printed in Singapore by KWF Printing Pte. Ltd.

contents >>

introduction >>

Soy beans or soya beans are rich natural foods that are highly versatile and can be used in their natural state, fermented to become miso and soy sauce, or made into flour or noodles. Soy beans easily absorb the flavours of other ingredients.

Soy beans belong to a species of legume that is indigenous to East Asia. Soy beans and soy products have been part of the Asian diet for many years. The soy bean was even recorded as one of the five 'sacred' grains during the time of the Zhou Dynasty (1050–256 B.C.), together with barley, wheat, millet and rice. Today, soy beans have become an important global crop, with America being a major world producer.

Nutritional Content

Soy beans are a good source of complete protein and are often consumed as a meat substitute. Soy beans also contain zinc, vitamin B, magnesium and isoflavones, which is a type of phytoestrogen believed to help in the prevention of cancer. Soy bean oil contains significant amounts of omega-3 fatty acids as well as mono-unsaturated and poly-unsaturated fatty acids, making it highly suitable for daily cooking. These special fat components are also believed to have beneficial effects in the prevention of cancer, in the improvement of rheumatoid arthritis and in the strengthening of the immune system.

Other soy products such as bean curd and soy milk are rich in soy protein, while soy flour is particularly high in dietary fibre and tempeh (fermented soy bean cake) provides vitamin B12. Soy bean sprouts also contain a lot of vitamin C.

Bean Curd

Bean curd is made by adding a coagulant to hot soy milk, which results in a smooth and pale curd that is bland in taste, but highly versatile. There are 3 types of fresh bean curd— firm, soft and silken. Firm bean curd contains less moisture than other types of bean curd and has a texture like that of meat. It is usually used in stir-fries or braised dishes. Soft bean curd has a smooth texture and is usually steamed, or used in soups. It is sometimes also mashed and used in meatballs or patties. Silken bean curd has a very delicate texture and is a typical feature in Japanese and Korean soups or stews.

Other bean curd products include deep-fried bean curd puffs and *abura-age*. Deep-fried bean curd puffs are golden brown in colour with a light, airy texture. They are used in soups and stews. *Abura-age* are thin, deep-fried slices of bean curd and are produced in Japan. These fried thin slices of bean curd are usually slit open and stuffed with vegetables or Japanese rice.

Soy Pastes and Soy Sauces

Soy pastes are made from salted fermented soy beans and are used mainly as condiments, in marinades or sauces. The salty pastes give added flavour and colour to stewed or braised dishes and to roasted meats. An example is hoisin sauce, a glossy, syrupy sauce that is used in Chinese dishes like Peking duck and barbecued pork.

Another kind of soy paste is miso, which is widely used in Japanese cuisine. Miso is made from combining steamed and crushed soy beans with barley and the optional ingredient of rice. Miso is used to give a rich flavour and creamy texture to soups and noodles.

Soy sauce or soya sauce is a fermented sauce made from soy beans, grains and salt. Soy sauces vary in taste and degrees of saltiness. The common Chinese light soy sauce has a salty, earthy flavour. It is mostly used to season food while cooking, or as a condiment at the table. Dark soy sauce is sweeter and less salty, and can be used to add colour to a dish. Store soy sauce in a cool place, away from direct sunlight.

The Japanese soy sauce (shoyu) is similar to Chinese light soy sauce. Japanese tamari, however, is made purely from soy beans, and as such is suitable for people with wheat allergies. This strongly flavoured sauce is commonly used as a sauce for raw fish or stews, soups and cooked meat dishes. Another thick soy sauce is Indonesian *kecap manis* which contains palm sugar, star anise and garlic.

Soy Beans and Soy Bean Sprouts

In their raw state, soy beans are toxic and must be thoroughly cooked before consuming. Yellow soy beans can be used as a soup base for clear stock. Soaking the soy beans before cooking helps to shorten the cooking time. Green soy beans, encased in pods, are known by the Japanese name, *edamame*. They are commonly boiled in salted water and eaten straight from their pods as an appetiser, or used in soups.

Tempeh is a fermented soy bean cake originating from Indonesia. The cooked soy beans are fermented with a rhizopus mould to create a compact white cake with a firm texture and nutty mushroom flavour. Tempeh is typically fried or used in soups, spreads, salads and sandwiches.

Sprouts from newly germinated soy beans are used as a vegetable. These fresh sprouts are popularly added raw to salads, and sandwiches to provide crispness and texture. Sprouts can also be briskly stir-fried or used in soups.

Bean Curd Skin and Soy Noodles

Bean curd skin is made from drying the layer of skin that forms from boiling soy milk. Bean curd skin is a good source of protein and calcium, and is available as sheets or sticks. Bean curd skin in sheet form is soft like fabric, and can be used as an edible wrapper for meat, seafood and vegetables.

Bean curd skin is also available in sticks, which are stiff and brittle. It is generally used in soups or desserts. If stored in a cool, dry place, the bean curd skin will keep indefinitely. Discard if it turns mouldy.

Fresh soy noodles are made from compressed bean curd, and may not be as easily available as dried soy noodles which are made from soy flour. Soy noodles have a chewy texture and are best enjoyed in salads or stir-fries.

Soy Milk and Soy Flour

Soy milk is cholestrol-free and lactose-free. It is commonly used as an alternative to dairy milk. Soy milk is often used as an ingredient in making breads, cakes, other baked goods and can be included in creams, sauces and soups. It can be enjoyed on its own or blended in smoothies and other beverages.

Soy flour is ground from roasted soy beans. It is gluten-free with a high protein content. Soy flour improves the colour, texture and moistness of baked goods, while imparting a subtle, pleasant soy flavour to the finished product.

bean curd

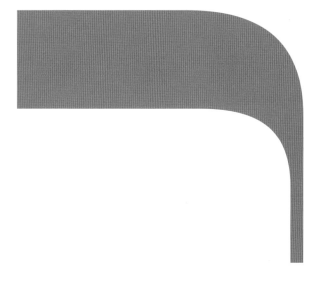

vegetables with bean curd dip

This healthy vegetarian dish is quick and easy to prepare. It is suitable for health-conscious individuals on the go.

Serves 6

Ingredients

Vegetables

Carrots	200 g (7 oz), peeled and cut into thick rounds
Broccoli	450 g (1 lb), cut into florets

Bean Curd Dip

Firm bean curd	300 g (10$\frac{1}{2}$ oz)
White miso	1$\frac{1}{2}$ Tbsp
White sesame seeds	1$\frac{1}{2}$ Tbsp, toasted and ground
White vinegar	85 ml (2$\frac{1}{2}$ fl oz / $\frac{1}{3}$ cup)
Olive oil	3 Tbsp

Garnish

White sesame seeds	1 tsp, toasted

Method

- Wrap bean curd in a clean tea towel and place on a plate. Place another plate on it to weigh it down. Refrigerate for 30 minutes to remove excess moisture.

- When bean curd is almost ready, bring a pot of lightly salted water to the boil. Add carrots and cook for 12–15 minutes or until carrots are tender. Add broccoli and cook for 5–6 minutes. Do not overcook. Drain well and set aside on a serving plate.

- Cut bean curd into cubes and place in a blender (food processor) together with remaining ingredients for dip . Purée until fine. Sprinkle toasted sesame seeds over dip and serve with carrots and broccoli.

curry vegetables
(sayur lodeh)

This is a dish that Malay and Indonesian food stalls commonly serve.
Serves 6

Ingredients

Cooking oil	4–6 Tbsp
Dried prawns (shrimps)	150 g (5$^1/_3$ oz), washed and ground
Coconut milk	1.25 litres (40 fl oz / 5 cups), ready-made or squeezed from 1 grated coconut with sufficient warm water added
Firm bean curd	300 g (10$^1/_2$ oz), cut into small pieces
Tempeh (fermented soy bean cakes)	2 pieces, cut into small squares
Salt	2 tsp

Spice Paste

Large red chillies	10–12
Shallots	10–12, peeled
Garlic	2 cloves, peeled
Dried prawn paste (*belacan*)	2.5-cm (1-in) piece, toasted
Candlenuts	6
Ground turmeric	1 tsp

Vegetables

Carrots	2, medium, peeled and cut into 5 x 1.5-cm (2 x $^3/_4$-in) strips
Yam bean (jicama)	300 g (10$^1/_2$ oz), peeled and cut into 5 x 1.5-cm (2 x $^3/_4$-in) strips
White cabbage leaves	$^1/_2$ medium-size head, core removed and leaves cut into 5-cm (2-in) squares
Aubergines (eggplants/ brinjals)	2, cut into rectangular pieces about 5-cm (2-in) long
Long beans	6, cut into 5-cm (2-in) lengths

Method

- Prepare spice paste. Place spice ingredients in a blender (food processor). Blend into a paste.

- Heat oil in a wok, add spice paste and stir-fry until fragrant. Add dried prawns and stir-fry until fragrant. Add more oil as necessary to prevent paste from burning and sticking to bottom of wok.

- Add coconut milk and bring to the boil.

- Add bean curd, tempeh and vegetables, then return mixture to the boil. Reduce heat to low and simmer until vegetables are tender.

- Season with salt and serve hot with rice.

bean curd and avocado dip

Serve this dip with crackers, bread sticks or vegetable sticks as a starter at cocktail parties.

Makes 1$\frac{1}{2}$ cups

Ingredients

Silken bean curd	300 g (10$\frac{1}{2}$ oz)
Ripe avocado	1, medium, peeled and mashed
Sour cream or mayonnaise	2 Tbsp
Salt	to taste
Lemon juice	1 tsp
Onion	1, small, peeled and finely chopped
Tabasco sauce	$\frac{1}{4}$ tsp or to taste
Cayenne pepper	$\frac{1}{4}$ tsp or to taste

Method

- Wrap bean curd in a clean tea towel and place on a plate. Place another plate on it to weigh it down. Refrigerate for 30 minutes to remove excess moisture.
- Mash bean curd, then mix well with mashed avocado. Mix in remaining ingredients and refrigerate until chilled before serving.

crispy fried bean curd cubes

These spicy bean curd cubes can be served as part of a meal or as a tasty appetiser.

Serves 4

Ingredients

Firm bean curd	600 g (1 lb 5$\frac{1}{3}$ oz)
Salt	1 tsp
Ground white pepper	$\frac{1}{8}$ tsp
Chinese five-spice powder	$\frac{1}{8}$ tsp
Breadcrumbs	150 g (5$\frac{1}{3}$ oz)
White sesame seeds	1 Tbsp
Plain (all-purpose) flour	55 g (2 oz)
Water	4 Tbsp
Cooking oil for deep-frying	

Method

- Wrap bean curd in a tea towel and place on a plate. Place another plate on it to weigh it down. Refrigerate for 30 minutes to remove excess moisture.
- Cut bean curd into large cubes, each about 3.5-cm (1$\frac{1}{2}$-in). Season with salt, pepper and five-spice powder.
- Combine breadcrumbs and sesame seeds.
- Mix flour and water together into a lumpy batter. Coat bean curd with batter, then coat with breadcrumb and sesame seed mixture.
- Heat oil for deep-frying and carefully lower bean curd cubes into hot oil. Deep-fry until golden brown. Serve with sweet chilli sauce, if desired.

abura-age with japanese rice

A well-loved Japanese favourite that is a meal in itself.

Serves 6–8

Ingredients

Abura-age (fried thin bean curd)	8
Water	1 litre (32 fl oz / 4 cups)
Dashi stock granules	3 tsp
Sugar	5 Tbsp
Shoyu	5 Tbsp

Japanese Rice

Japanese short-grained rice	400 g (14$^1/_3$ oz)
Water	500 ml (16 fl oz / 2 cups)
Japanese rice vinegar	3$^1/_2$ Tbsp
Sugar	8 tsp
Salt	1 tsp
White sesame seeds	2 Tbsp, lightly toasted

Method

- Prepare Japanese rice. Rinse rice until the water runs clear. Drain rice in a sieve for 1 hour. Cook rice and 500ml water in a rice cooker. When rice is done, transfer to a large, wet mixing bowl.

- Combine rice vinegar, sugar and salt in a small bowl and stir until sugar and salt dissolve. Sprinkle mixture evenly over rice, together with sesame seeds, then use a wet spatula to fold mixture and sesame seeds into rice. Leave rice to cool.

- Lightly blanch *abura-age* to remove excess oil, then drain well and place on a tea towel. Cut each *abura-age* in half, then carefully pry apart at cut end.

- Bring 1 litre water to the boil in a pot and stir in dashi granules and sugar. Reduce heat and place *abura-age* into pot. Simmer for 25–30 minutes, then add shoyu. Continue to simmer until almost all the liquid evaporates. Place *abura-age* in a sieve to drain and set aside.

- Wet your hands and shape rice into 16 rectangular parcels, small enough to fill *abura-age* bags. Fill an *abura-age* bag carefully with a rice parcel. Repeat with remaining parcels. Serve immediately.

For a more authentic Japanese flavour, serve with wasabi, pickled ginger and shoyu on the side.

abura-age with spring onions

Abura-age can be filled and eaten on its own or used as a meat substitute in soups and oden (hotpot) dishes. Here, it is deliciously paired with a light vegetarian filling.

Serves 4–6

Ingredients

Abura-age (fried thin bean curd) 4

Filling

Spring onions (scallions)	8, finely chopped
Shoyu	2 Tbsp
Garlic	2 cloves, peeled and finely chopped
White sesame seeds	3 Tbsp, lightly toasted

Method

- Lightly blanch *abura-age* to remove excess oil, then drain well and place on a tea towel.
- Cut each *abura-age* in half, then carefully pry apart at cut end.
- Combine ingredients for filling and divide into 8 portions. Spoon into bags and grill for 2–3 minutes on each side until crisp and lightly brown.
- Serve hot.

cabbage and bean curd patties

This makes for a wonderful little snack with a cup of Chinese tea.
Serves 4

Ingredients

Chinese cabbage	450 g (1 lb)
Salt	2 tsp
Soft bean curd	300 g (10$\frac{1}{2}$ oz)
Minced pork	200 g (7 oz)
Cooking oil	
for frying	

Dough

Plain (all-purpose) flour	750 g (1 lb 10$\frac{1}{2}$ oz)
Boiling water	625 ml (20 fl oz / 2$\frac{1}{2}$ cups)

Seasoning

Light soy sauce	$\frac{1}{2}$ Tbsp
Sugar	$\frac{1}{2}$ Tbsp
Ground white pepper	1 tsp
Corn flour (cornstarch)	1 Tbsp
Sesame oil	$\frac{1}{2}$ Tbsp

Method

- Prepare dough. Place flour in a large bowl and add boiling water. Stir to mix thoroughly, but do not start to knead into dough yet. Cover bowl with a clean, damp cloth and leave for 10 minutes.

- Knead mixture into a rough dough. Dough should feel damp but not wet. Add more water as necessary. Remove from bowl and cover dough with a clean, damp cloth. Leave for 20 minutes.

- Knead dough until smooth for about 15–20 minutes. Cover with a clean, damp cloth until needed.

- Wash and drain cabbage, then rub leaves with salt. Set aside for 10 minutes. Wash off salt, gently squeeze out excess water and slice cabbage finely.

- Mash bean curd, then mix with cabbage, pork and seasoning ingredients. Divide into 8 portions.

- Divide dough into 8 portions, then roll each portion into a circle about 10-cm (4-in) in diameter. Spoon 1 portion of filling onto the centre of a dough circle, then bring edges of dough up to enclose filling. Repeat until ingredients are used up. Flatten patties slightly with a rolling pin.

- Heat oil in a frying pan and cook patties for about 10 minutes on each side. Serve hot.

meatballs in tomato sauce

Adding soft bean curd to the minced beef makes this a healthy yet tasty variation to regular meatballs.

Makes 25–30 meatballs

Ingredients

Minced beef	450 g (16 oz / 1 lb)
Soft bean curd	150 g (5$\frac{1}{3}$ oz), mashed
Egg	1, beaten
Onion	1, peeled and finely chopped
Garlic	2 cloves, peeled and finely chopped
Chopped parsley	1 Tbsp
Salt	to taste
Ground black pepper	to taste
Cooking oil	2 Tbsp

Sauce

Tomato sauce	500 g (1 lb 1$\frac{1}{2}$ oz)
Water	435 ml (14 fl oz / 1$\frac{3}{4}$ cups)
Onion	1, peeled and cut into cubes

Method

- Combine all ingredients except oil and sauce ingredients in a mixing bowl and mix well. Shape into balls about 4-cm (1$\frac{1}{2}$-in) in diameter.
- Heat oil in a non-stick pan and over medium-high heat. Fry meatballs until light brown all over.
- Combine tomato sauce and water and pour into pan over meatballs. Add onion and simmer for at least 20 minutes. Taste and adjust seasoning with salt and pepper. Serve warm.

spicy bean curd with minced pork

This popular dish is more commonly known as Ma Po Tofu, and is served at Chinese restaurants all over the world.

Serves 4

Ingredients

Cooking oil	3 Tbsp
Garlic	2 cloves, peeled and chopped
Minced pork	200 g (7 oz)
Spicy bean paste	2 Tbsp
Black bean paste	2½ tsp
Chilli powder	1 tsp
Salt	1 tsp
Light soy sauce	2 tsp
Ginger	2.5-cm (1-in) knob, peeled and grated
Soft bean curd	300 g (10½ oz), cut into 2.5-cm (1-in) squares
Corn flour (cornstarch)	2 Tbsp, mixed with 2 Tbsp water
Spring onion (scallion)	1, chopped

Method

- Heat oil in a wok and stir-fry garlic until lightly fragrant.
- Add minced pork and cook for 1–2 minutes until pork changes colour and is lightly cooked.
- Add bean pastes, chilli powder, salt, soy sauce, ginger and bean curd. Stir-fry lightly, so as not to break up bean curd. Sprinkle in some water to make it easier to stir and prevent contents of wok from burning. Bring mixture to the boil.
- Reduce heat and simmer for 5 minutes. Add corn flour mixture and spring onion. Dish out and serve hot with rice.

prawn, capsicum and bean curd kebabs

These kebabs are easy to do, making them great for barbecues.
Makes 6 kebabs

Ingredients

Prawns (shrimps)	12, large, peeled and deveined
Yellow capsicum (bell pepper)	1, small, cored and cut into 12 squares, each 2.5-cm (1-in)
Firm bean curd	70 g (2½ oz), cut into 6 cubes, each 2.5-cm (1-in)
Salt	to taste

Marinade

Pineapple juice	4 Tbsp
Honey	2 Tbsp
Brown sugar	1 tsp
Bamboo skewers	6, soaked in water for 20 minutes

Method

- Combine ingredients for marinade in a bowl. Add prawns, capsicum and bean curd, then leave refrigerated for 1 hour.
- Thread 2 prawns, 2 capsicum squares and 1 bean curd cube alternately on each skewer. Reserve marinade.
- Sprinkle kebabs with salt to taste. Bake kebabs at 180°C (350°F) or grill kebabs, basting with reserved marinade, until prawns turn pink and are cooked. Serve hot.

fish cakes with bean curd

These fish cakes combine the goodness of fish and bean curd in fragrant, golden brown patties.

Serves 4

Ingredients

Firm fish fillet	450 g (1 lb), without skin, coarsely chopped
Firm bean curd	200 g (7 oz), mashed
Onion	1, peeled and finely chopped
Garlic	2 cloves, peeled and finely chopped
Plain (all-purpose) flour	70 g (2¹/₂ oz) + extra for dusting
Salt	to taste
Ground black pepper	to taste
Cooking oil	

Method

- Combine all ingredients except plain flour for dusting and oil. Divide mixture into 6 portions and shape each portion into a large, flat pattie. Dust with flour.

- Heat 2 Tbsp oil in a pan over medium heat. Pan-fry patties for 5 minutes on each side or until golden brown and crispy. Serve hot with chilli sauce or tartar sauce.

fudgy walnut brownies

This is another fat-reduced option to a sweet dessert. These brownies require less butter than regular brownies and are just as delicious!

Ingredients

Silken bean curd	180 g (6$\frac{1}{3}$ oz), mashed
Vegetable oil	4 Tbsp
Castor (superfine) sugar	400 g (14$\frac{1}{3}$ oz)
Semi-sweet chocolate	110 g (4 oz), chopped and melted
Vanilla essence	1 tsp
Plain (all-purpose) flour	85 g (3 oz)
Cocoa powder	30 g (1 oz)
Bicarbonate of soda	$\frac{1}{4}$ tsp
Salt	$\frac{1}{8}$ tsp
Semi-sweet chocolate chips	85 g (3 oz)
Chopped walnuts	100 g (3$\frac{1}{2}$ oz)

Method

- Preheat oven to 180°C (350°F). Line a 20-cm (8-in) square baking tin and set aside.

- In a large mixing bowl, combine bean curd, oil and sugar. Add melted chocolate and vanilla essence.

- Sift flour, cocoa powder, bicarbonate of soda and salt into a separate bowl. Add gradually to bean curd mixture. Fold lightly to combine. Add chocolate chips, then walnuts.

- Pour brownie batter into baking tin and spread evenly. Bake for 30 minutes. Remove from oven and leave to cool. Remove from tin and cut into squares to serve.

soy pastes
& soy sauces

chinese noodles in special sauce

La mian is made fresh at Chinese restaurants and eateries in Beijing.
Serves 4

Ingredients

La mian	600 g (1 lb 5⅓ oz)
Sesame oil	2 Tbsp
Cooking oil	5 Tbsp
Spring onions (scallions)	2, minced
Minced pork	200 g (7 oz)
Carrots	2, medium, peeled and diced
Cucumber	½, small, peeled and cut into thin shreds

Seasoning

Yellow bean paste	2 Tbsp
Sweet bean paste	2 Tbsp
Dark soy sauce	½ Tbsp
Sugar	½ Tbsp

Method

- Bring a large pot of water to the boil and blanch noodles for 2 minutes. Drain thoroughly and add sesame oil to prevent noodles from sticking.
- Heat cooking oil in a wok over medium heat and add spring onions and all the seasoning ingredients. Stir-fry for 1 minute.
- Add minced pork and carrots and cook for 3–4 minutes until sauce mixture is bubbling. Pour sauce over noodles.
- Serve with cucumber shreds.

If fresh *la mian* is not available, use the dried variety. Prepare them according to the manufacturer's directions.

stir-fried capsicums in miso sauce

Although simple, this dish is tasty and rich in vitamin C.
Serves 4

Ingredients

Capsicums (bell peppers)	4, medium, combination of red, yellow and green
Shoyu	4 Tbsp
Sake	4 Tbsp
Mirin	4 Tbsp
Sugar	1½ Tbsp
Miso	3 Tbsp
Water	3 Tbsp
Cooking oil	2 Tbsp
Red chilli	1, seeded and sliced

Method

- Cut capsicums in half and remove seeds. Cut into long, thin strips. Set aside.
- Combine shoyu, sake, mirin and sugar in a small bowl.
- Mix miso with water to form a paste.
- Heat oil in a wok and add capsicums and chilli. Stir-fry for 6 minutes until capsicums are lightly cooked.
- Reduce heat and add shoyu mixture. Cook, stirring, for 2 minutes.
- Add miso paste and stir to mix well. Cook for another 2 minutes before serving hot with rice.

miso soup

This rich, salty soup is traditionally consumed for breakfast in Japan. It is also served with other dishes in a Japanese meal.

Ingredients

Dried wakame	10 g (1/3 oz)
Water	435 ml (14 fl oz / 1 3/4 cups)
Dashi stock granules	1 tsp
Miso	2 Tbsp
Soft bean curd	300 g (10 1/2 oz), cut into small cubes

Method

- Soak wakame in cold water for 15 minutes. Drain, then cut into squares, approximately 2.5-cm (1-in). Set aside.

- Combine water and dashi stock granules in a pot and bring to the boil. Reduce heat and allow soup to simmer.

- Place miso into a small bowl and add 4–5 Tbsp dashi stock. Stir to dissolve miso, then add 2–3 Tbsp to the pot. Taste and add more miso if required. Add wakame and bean curd, then increase heat and return soup to the boil.

- Serve hot as part of a Japanese meal.

salmon teriyaki

Teriyaki refers to a sweet soy sauce marinade that the Japanese popularly use for broiled or grilled meats. It is made using the 4 basic ingredients of shoyu, sake, mirin and sugar.

Serves 4

Ingredients

Salmon	4 fillets, each about 140 g (5 oz), with skin

Teriyaki Marinade

Shoyu	4 Tbsp
Sake	4 Tbsp
Mirin	4 Tbsp
Sugar	1½ Tbsp

Method

- Combine ingredients for teriyaki marinade.
- Place salmon in a shallow dish and pour marinade over. Refrigerate for 30 minutes.
- Remove salmon from marinade and place on a baking tray. Reserve marinade.
- Grill salmon for 5 minutes, then turn it over and grill other side for another 5 minutes.
- Brush salmon with marinade and grill until marinade bubbles. Turn salmon over and repeat to marinate, then grill other side until marinade bubbles.
- Remove salmon from tray and place on serving plates, being careful not to flake flesh.
- Serve hot.

NOTE

For a complete Japanese meal, serve with Japanese rice (see p 20 for preparation of Japanese rice).

fish slices in soy sauce

This braised method of cooking is a healthy alternative to deep-frying fish. The sauce also goes very well with plain white rice.

Serves 4

Ingredients

Fish steak (eg. cod, mullet, snapper)	600 g (1lb 5½ oz), cut into 0.5-cm (¼-in) thick slices
Salt	1 tsp
Ground white pepper	to taste
Corn flour (cornstarch)	1 Tbsp
Cooking oil	2 Tbsp
Ginger	3 thin slices, peeled
Spring onions (scallions)	2, cut into 2.5-cm (1-in) lengths
Light soy sauce	3 Tbsp
Water	2 Tbsp
Sugar	1 tsp

Method

- Season fish with salt and pepper, then dust with corn flour.
- Heat oil in a wok and add ginger and spring onions. Cook lightly for about 30 seconds. Add fish slices one at a time. This will prevent the fish from clumping together. Cook for 1–2 minutes.
- Add soy sauce, water and sugar and bring to the boil. Stir-fry for 2–3 minutes and remove from heat. Serve hot with rice.

baked chicken teriyaki

This popular Japanese dish is tasty and also healthy because it is baked without oil.

Serves 4

Ingredients

Chicken meat	4 breasts, skinned and cut into cubes
Honey	1¹/₂ Tbsp

Marinade

Ginger	3-cm (1¹/₂-in) knob, peeled and grated
Shoyu	6 Tbsp
Salt	to taste
Ground white pepper	to taste
Garlic	1 clove, peeled and crushed
Sake or white wine	6 Tbsp

Method

- Mix chicken with honey until well coated.
- Combine marinade ingredients in a porcelain or glass bowl and add chicken. Mix well, then cover and refrigerate for 2 hours, giving chicken a stir occasionally.
- Heat oven to 180°C (350°F) and line a deep baking tin with aluminium foil. Arrange chicken pieces in a single layer in tin. Pour marinade over chicken and bake for 20 minutes or until chicken is cooked through and tender. Baste chicken with juices in tin every 6 minutes.
- Remove chicken from oven. Using a slotted spoon, transfer chicken to a serving plate and pour cooking juices into a small bowl to accompany chicken . Serve with white rice.

spicy
soy sauce
chicken

This is an adaptation of a popular Indonesian dish..
Serves 4–6

Ingredients

Salt	1 tsp
White wine vinegar	3 Tbsp
Soft brown sugar	1 Tbsp
Chicken	1, about 1.3 kg (3 lb), cut into 10–12 even-size pieces
Cooking oil	2 Tbsp

Sauce

Onion	1, peeled and finely chopped
Green chilli	1, seeded and finely chopped
Garlic	2 cloves, peeled
Water	250 ml (8 fl oz / 1 cup)
White wine vinegar	1 Tbsp
Light soy sauce	2 Tbsp
Sugar	1 Tbsp
Tomatoes	4, medium-size, blanched, peeled, seeded and chopped

Method

- Combine salt, vinegar and brown sugar in a large mixing bowl. Add chicken and mix well to coat chicken, then set aside in the refrigerator for 30 minutes.

- Prepare sauce. Place all ingredients except tomatoes in a blender (food processor) and blend at high speed until mixture is smooth. Set aside.

- In a large frying pan, heat oil over medium heat. Add marinated chicken and fry for 10–15 minutes, turning chicken pieces over occasionally until golden brown all over. Remove from heat and drain well on absorbent paper.

- Using the same pan, add sauce and bring to a boil. Add chicken and tomatoes. Reduce heat to low, cover and cook for 20–25 minutes. Remove cover and cook for another 10 minutes, stirring constantly, until liquid is reduced by one-third.

- Remove from heat and serve immediately.

stewed soy sauce duck with yam

The creamy flesh of the cooked yam absorbs the juicy goodness of the stewed duck in this dish and makes it particularly flavourful.

Serves 4

Ingredients

Duck	1/2, large, about 600 g (1 lb 5 1/3 oz)
Yam (taro)	450 g (1 lb)
Cooking oil for deep-frying	
Spring onions (scallions)	3, sliced
Water	625 ml (20 fl oz / 2 1/2 cups)

Marinade

Light soy sauce	4 Tbsp
Ginger wine	2 Tbsp (see p 57)
Sugar	2 tsp

Seasoning

Light soy sauce	2 Tbsp
Sugar	1 tsp
Salt	1/2 tsp
Ground white pepper	1/2 tsp

Method

- Clean and rinse duck. Pat dry, then cut into bite-size pieces.
- Mix together marinade ingredients in a large bowl, then add duck and leave refrigerated for 30 minutes. Drain duck and reserve marinade.
- Soak yam in boiling water for 10 minutes, then peel. Cut into large chunks.
- Heat oil for deep-frying in a wok over medium heat and cook yam for 5 minutes. Remove with a slotted spoon.
- Drain all but 2 Tbsp oil from wok and reheat over medium heat. Stir-fry duck for 3 minutes and remove.
- Add another 4 Tbsp oil to wok and stir-fry spring onions for a few seconds. Return duck to wok and add reserved marinade, yam, seasoning ingredients and water. Bring to the boil, then reduce heat and simmer for 30 minutes until duck is tender.
- Serve hot with rice.

chinese barbecued pork

Although the minimum marinating time for the pork is 2 hours, leaving it overnight allows the pork to absorb the flavours more thoroughly, resulting in a truly tasty dish.

Serves 4

Ingredients

Lean pork fillet	900 g (2 lb), trimmed of excess fat and cut into 4 pieces
Honey	2 tsp

Marinade

Light soy sauce	2 Tbsp
Dry sherry	2 Tbsp
Sesame oil	2 tsp
Hoisin sauce	2 Tbsp
Soft brown sugar	55 g (2 oz)
Garlic	1 clove, peeled and crushed

Method

- Combine ingredients for marinade.

- Place pork in a non-metallic container and pour marinade over. Cover and leave refrigerated for at least 2 hours or overnight.

- Heat oven to 180°C (350°F). Drain pork and reserve marinade. Place pork on a wire rack in a roasting tin filled with water up to 1-cm ($\frac{1}{2}$-in) high. Cook for 20 minutes.

- Remove pork from oven and dip into reserved marinade. Return pork to rack and cook for another 20–25 minutes or until meat is tender.

- Brush pork with honey to give it an attractive glaze and allow meat to cool slightly. Slice and serve hot or at room temperature with rice.

hot pork paste

This traditional Chinese dish is served with other dishes as an accompaniment to plain rice or porridge.

Serves 4–6

Ingredients

Lean minced pork	700 g (1 lb)
Cooking oil	2 Tbsp
Red chilli	1, seeded and finely chopped

Seasoning

Cayenne pepper	1 Tbsp
Hot bean sauce	1 Tbsp
Sugar	2 Tbsp
Light soy sauce	3 Tbsp
Salt	1 tsp
Ginger wine*	1 Tbsp

*Ginger Wine

Ginger	5-cm (2-in) knob, peeled and shredded
Chinese cooking wine	250 ml (8 fl oz / 1 cup)

Method

- Prepare ginger wine. Place ginger and wine in a clean, screw top jar. Cover and leave to stand for at least 1 hour before using. Ginger wine will keep indefinitely, if kept refrigerated.
- Place pork in a bowl and add seasoning. Mix well.
- Heat oil in a wok. Add pork mixture and stir-fry over high heat for 3 minutes, breaking up any lumps of meat.
- Add chilli and stir-fry for another 2–3 minutes until pork is well cooked.
- Remove and garnish with sliced chilli if desired before serving.

braised pork with bean curd puffs

Braising softens the belly pork and gives it a lovely melting texture. The resulting sauce is also rich and flavourful.

Serves 4–6

Ingredients

Belly pork	800 g (1¾ lb), cut into 4 equal strips
Dark soy sauce	2 Tbsp
Cooking oil	for deep-frying
Light soy sauce	3 Tbsp
Ginger	4 thin slices, peeled
Fried bean curd puffs	8–10
Water	500 ml (16 fl oz / 2 cups)
Sugar	1 Tbsp
Star anise	4
Cassia	1 stick, about 7.5-cm (3-in) long
Salt	to taste

Method

- Immerse pork in boiling water for 3–5 minutes to remove any impurities. Drain well. Rub pork with dark soy sauce.

- Heat oil in a wok over medium heat, then fry pork for 3 minutes. Drain.

- Place pork in a casserole and pour light soy sauce over. Add ginger, bean curd puffs, water, sugar, star anise and cassia and bring to the boil over medium heat. Turn pork over from time to time to ensure even cooking.

- When mixture comes to the boil, reduce heat, cover and simmer for 45 minutes until pork is tender and sauce is reduced.

- Season to taste with salt, then remove from heat and serve hot with rice.

steamed spare ribs with black beans

It takes some skill to cut the spare ribs into the short lengths needed in this recipe. Ask the butcher to do it for you. Choose meaty ribs to really enjoy this dish.

Serves 4–6

Ingredients

Pork spare ribs	800 g (1¼ lb), cut into 3-cm (1-in) lengths
Cooking oil	2 Tbsp
Shallots	2, peeled and chopped
Garlic	2 cloves, peeled and crushed
Salted black beans	2 Tbsp, soaked for 5 minutes, then drain and crushed
Salt	1 tsp
Water	2 Tbsp
Sugar	2 tsp
Light soy sauce	1 Tbsp
Red chilli	1, seeded and sliced
Corn flour (cornstarch)	1 Tbsp, mixed with 1 Tbsp water

Method

- Immerse pork ribs in boiling water for 2 minutes to remove any impurities. Drain well and place on a deep steaming plate.
- Heat oil in a wok and stir-fry shallots and garlic until lightly fragrant. Add black beans, salt, water, sugar, soy sauce and chilli and stir-fry to mix. Allow mixture to come to the boil, then stir in corn flour mixture and quickly pour mixture over pork ribs. Toss well together.
- Place steaming plate in a steamer and cook for 25–30 minutes until ribs are well done. A skewer should pierce through the thickest part of flesh easily. Garnish as desired and serve hot

chinese-style steak

Using soy sauce to marinate beef gives it a distinctively rich flavour. The natural taste of the beef is also retained for maximum enjoyment.

Serves 4

Ingredients

Rump or sirloin steak	4 slices, each about 200 g (7 oz)
Butter	4 Tbsp

Marinade

Dark soy sauce	2 Tbsp
Light soy sauce	1 Tbsp
Garlic	2 cloves, peeled and chopped
Freshly cracked black pepper	$1\frac{1}{2}$ tsp
Sugar	2 tsp
Ginger wine	1 Tbsp (see p 57)
Cooking oil	2 Tbsp
Corn flour (cornstarch)	1 tsp
Water	85 ml ($2\frac{1}{2}$ fl oz / $\frac{1}{3}$ cup)

Method

- Tenderise beef by beating it lightly with the spine of a cleaver.
- Combine ingredients for marinade in a large bowl. Add beef and refrigerate for 1 hour.
- Heat 1 Tbsp butter in a frying pan and add a slice of beef. Cook each side over medium heat until both sides are browned. Repeat to cook remaining slices of beef. Remove and serve.

soy beans &
soy bean sprouts

homemade
soy milk

Soy milk is easy to prepare and makes a nutritious drink. It can be served both hot or cold.

Makes about 1.2 litres (40 fl oz / 5 cups)

Ingredients

Soy beans	150 g (5$\frac{1}{3}$ oz), soaked for 6 hours
Water	1.5 litres (48 fl oz / 6 cups)
Sugar	125 g (4$\frac{1}{2}$ oz) or to taste

Method

- Drain and place soy beans in a blender (food processor) with 500 ml (16 fl oz / 2 cups) water. Blend into a smooth pulp.
- Pour pulp into a muslin bag or cloth strainer with remaining water and squeeze to obtain milk. Discard dry pulp.
- Heat soy milk in a saucepan and bring to the boil. Stir in sugar and return milk to the boil. Remove from heat and serve hot or leave to cool before refrigerating to serve cold. Soy milk can be stored refrigerated for up to 3 days.

cooked
soy beans

If canned soy beans are not available, prepare your own using the easily available dried soy beans. These beans are seldom eaten on their own, but used as an ingredient in other recipes.

Makes about 2$\frac{1}{2}$ cups

Ingredients

Dried soy beans   225 g (8 oz)

Method

- Pick over soy beans, then rinse well and drain. Soak in 750 ml (24 fl oz / 3 cups) water for 8–12 hours.
- Drain and rinse soaked beans, then weigh. Use 4.5 litres (152 fl oz / 18 cups) of water for every 450 g (1 lb) soaked beans. Place beans in a large pot with fresh water and bring to the boil. Reduce heat and simmer for about 3 hours or until beans are tender.
- Use as needed. Store in small amounts in individual freezer bags or containers in the freezer.

soy bean minestrone

This Italian soup used to be made with whatever vegetables were in season. Today, it is popularly made with beans, onions, tomatoes, celery and carrots. Pasta is sometimes also added.

Serves 6–8

Ingredients

Olive oil	2 Tbsp
Onion	1, large, peeled and finely chopped
Celery	2 stalks, cut into 1-cm (1/2-in) squares
Carrot	1, large, peeled and diced
Garlic	3 cloves, peeled and finely chopped
Tomatoes	3, peeled, seeded and diced
Water	2 litres (64 fl oz / 8 cups)
Finely chopped fresh oregano	3 Tbsp
Finely chopped fresh thyme	2 Tbsp
Finely chopped fresh rosemary	1 Tbsp
Cooked soy beans (see p 69)	280 g (10 oz)
Pasta in small shapes	140 g (5 oz)
Salt	to taste
Ground black pepper	to taste

Garnish
Parsley

Method

- Heat oil in a large saucepan over medium heat. Sauté onion, celery and carrot for 8–10 minutes or until onion is soft and translucent.

- Add garlic and sauté for another 5 minutes. Add tomatoes and water and bring to the boil.

- Reduce heat and add oregano, thyme and rosemary. Simmer until vegetables are tender, about 12 minutes.

- Add soy beans, pasta and cook until pasta is al dente. Season to taste with salt and pepper. Garnish with parsley and serve immediately.

soy bean pita

This recipe offers an excellent alternative to the usual meat-filled pitas.
The soy beans add bite and are a wonderful source of protein

Serves 4

Ingredients

Cooking oil	2 Tbsp
Onions	2, peeled and chopped
Garlic	2 cloves, peeled and chopped
Green capsicum (bell pepper)	1, seeded and cut into small squares
Tomatoes	2, seeded and cut into small cubes
Cooked soy beans (see p 69)	400 g (14$\frac{1}{3}$ oz)
Water	125 ml (4 fl oz / $\frac{1}{2}$ cup)
Tomato paste	150 g (5$\frac{1}{3}$ oz)
Chilli powder	$\frac{1}{2}$ tsp
Salt	$\frac{1}{2}$ tsp or to taste
Pita breads	4
Lettuce	12 leaves, finely shredded
Cheddar or mozzarella cheese	to taste, grated

Method

- Heat oil in a frying pan over medium heat. Add onions and garlic, then cook until fragrant but not brown. Add capsicum and cook for 5–8 minutes until just tender.

- Add tomatoes and soy beans, followed by water, tomato paste and chilli powder. Mix well. Add salt and remove from heat.

- Toast pita bread, then cut each one in half. Fill with shredded lettuce and soy bean filling. Sprinkle with cheese and serve immediately.

NOTE

Pita bread is available from supermarkets. It can be eaten plain, with olive oil or stuffed with various fillings and eaten as a sandwich. It can also be topped with spreads and meats. (see p 89).

boiled edamame

Often served in Japanese restaurants, boiled edamame are not only nutritious, but simple to prepare! Serve the beans in their pods and simply squeeze the beans out of the pods when eating.

Serves 4

Ingredients

Whole *edamame*   225 g (¹/₂ lb), rinsed
Salt   1 Tbsp

Method

• Bring a large pot of water to the boil. Add *edamame* and cook for 5–10 minutes. Drain and sprinkle salt over. Serve.

soy bean and vegetable curry

Using soy milk makes this curry a healthy, yet tasty option to the usual coconut milk-based curries.

Serves 4–6

Ingredients

Cooking oil	2 Tbsp (to taste, add more if necessary)
Onion	1, peeled and chopped
Garlic	2 cloves, peeled and crushed
Vegetable curry paste	2 Tbsp
Soy milk	250 ml (8 fl oz / 1 cup)
Carrots	2, medium, peeled and cut into chunks
Broccoli	150 g (5$\frac{1}{3}$ oz), cut into small florets
Cooked soy beans (see p 69)	400 g (14$\frac{1}{3}$ oz)
Salt	1 tsp
Corn flour (cornstarch)	$\frac{1}{2}$ Tbsp, mixed with 1 Tbsp water

Method

- Heat oil in a large saucepan over medium heat. Add onion, garlic and curry paste and sauté until golden.
- Add soy milk and carrots and simmer until carrots are tender.
- Add broccoli and soy beans and continue to simmer over low heat until broccoli is tender. Season with salt, then stir in corn flour mixture and cook until curry is lightly thickened.
- Serve hot with rice.

sausage and bean hotpot

A combination of soy and kidney beans is used in this recipe. Feel free to omit or substitute the type and amount of beans as desired.

Serves 4

Ingredients

Cooking oil	3 Tbsp
Onion	1, peeled and chopped
Garlic	2 cloves, peeled and crushed
Good quality pork sausages	450 g (1 lb), each cut in half
Canned red kidney beans	110 g (4 oz), drained
Cooked soy beans (see p 69)	110 g (4 oz)
Tomato paste	2 Tbsp
Salt	to taste
Freshly cracked black pepper	to taste

Garnish
Parsley

Method

- Heat oil in a heavy-based pan and lightly sauté onion and garlic for about 5 minutes.
- Add sausages and cook for about 10 minutes until sausages are lightly browned.
- Add beans, tomato paste and enough water to cover ingredients. Simmer gently for 15 minutes, stirring occasionally and adding more water if needed. Check that the sausages are cooked thoroughly.
- Taste and season with salt and pepper if necessary.
- Garnish with parsley and serve hot.

soy bean patties

These tasty patties use soy beans as a substitute for meat.

Serves 4

Ingredients

Cooking oil for frying

Patties

Cooked soy beans (see p 69)	280 g (10 oz)
Onion	1, peeled and finely chopped
Tomato paste	1 Tbsp
Chilli sauce	1½ tsp
Chopped parsley	1 Tbsp
Wholemeal breadcrumbs	280 g (10 oz)

Coating

Egg	1, beaten
Milk	1 Tbsp
Plain (all-purpose) flour	100 g (3½ oz)
Japanese breadcrumbs	280 g (10 oz)

Method

- Mash beans, then mix well with onion, tomato paste, chilli sauce, parsley and wholemeal breadcrumbs. Divide mixture into 8 even portions. Using your hands, roll each portion into a ball and flatten into a patty.

- Combine egg and milk in a bowl. Place flour and breadcrumbs separately in deep plates. Coat patties lightly with flour, then dip in egg mixture before coating with Japanese breadcrumbs.

- Heat some oil in a frying pan over medium heat. Cook patties 2–3 at a time until golden brown on both sides. Drain on absorbent paper.

- Serve, garnished as desired.

flowering chives with soy bean sprouts

This simple and nutritious dish can be served as part of a Chinese meal with white rice.

Serves 4

Ingredients

Flowering chives	55 g (2 oz)
Soy bean sprouts	300 g (10½ oz)
Cooking oil	2 Tbsp
Chopped garlic	½ Tbsp
Salt	½ tsp
Light soy sauce	1 Tbsp
Ground white pepper	½ tsp

Method

• Trim ends of chives and discard any yellowing stems. Wash, then cut chives into 2.5-cm (1-in) lengths.

• Pluck tails of soy bean sprouts, then wash and drain well in a colander.

• Heat oil in a wok and fry garlic until fragrant. Do not allow garlic to burn. Add chives and soy bean sprouts, then salt, soy sauce and pepper. Stir-fry over high heat for about 1 minute. Do not overcook the soy bean sprouts.

• Remove from heat and serve immediately.

tempeh in sweet soy sauce

Tempeh has a lovely nutty flavour and is delicious when fried and coated with a sweet dark sauce.

Serves 4

Ingredients

Cooking oil	for deep-frying
Tempeh (fermented soy bean cake)	350 g (12$\frac{1}{2}$ oz), cut into even-sized strips
Shallots	45 g (1$\frac{1}{2}$ oz), peeled and chopped
Garlic	45 g (1$\frac{1}{2}$ oz), peeled and chopped
Galangal	30 g (1 oz), peeled and sliced
Large red chillies	30 g (1 oz), seeded and finely sliced
Palm sugar	15 g ($\frac{1}{2}$ oz), chopped
Sweet soy sauce	2 Tbsp
Water	2 Tbsp
Tomato	1, peeled, seeded and cut into strips
Salt	to taste

Method

- Heat cooking oil in a wok over medium heat. Carefully lower tempeh strips into hot oil and fry until light golden and crisp. Remove and drain well.

- Leaving 2 Tbsp oil in wok, sauté shallots, garlic, galangal and chillies until lightly fragrant. Add palm sugar, sweet soy sauce and water. Return mixture to the boil.

- Add tomato and tempeh strips, then cook until sauce is reduced and thickened.

- Season to taste with salt and serve hot with rice.

NOTE

You can omit the palm sugar and relace the sweet soy sauce with 2 Tbsp of *kecap manis* if desired.

citrus salad with soy bean sprouts

The soy bean sprouts add extra crunch to this tangy and refreshing salad.

Serves 4

Ingredients

Butterhead lettuce	1 head
Soy bean sprouts	300 g (10½ oz), tailed
Grapefruit	2, large, red or pink, peeled and segmented
Navel oranges	2, peeled and segmented
Kiwi fruit	4, peeled and cut into quarters

Dressing

Olive oil	4 Tbsp
Freshly squeezed orange juice	3 Tbsp
Balsamic vinegar	3 Tbsp
Honey	1 Tbsp
Cracked black pepper	¼ tsp

Method

- Arrange lettuce leaves in a salad bowl, then add soy bean sprouts and fruit on top.
- In small bowl, whisk together olive oil, orange juice, vinegar, honey and pepper.
- Drizzle desired amount of dressing over salad.
- Serve immediately.

pizza with tempeh

This recipe adds a new dimension to tempeh by using it as a pizza topping. Serve this vegetarian pizza as an alternative to your usual pizza.

Serves 4

Ingredients

Pita breads	4

Pizza Sauce

Vegetable oil	2 Tbsp
Onion	1, peeled and finely chopped
Garlic	2 cloves, peeled and crushed
Red capsicum (bell pepper)	1, seeded and finely chopped
Tomato purée	300 g (10$\frac{1}{2}$ oz)
Broccoli	450 g (1 lb), cut into small florets
Dried oregano	$\frac{1}{2}$ tsp
Salt	to taste
Ground white pepper	to taste
Button mushrooms	140 g (5 oz), sliced
Tempeh (fermented soy bean cake)	280 g (10 oz), cut into small cubes
Light soy sauce	2 Tbsp
Vegetable oil	4 Tbsp
Tomatoes	2, chopped

Method

- Prepare pizza sauce. Heat oil over medium heat and add onion, garlic and capsicum. Stir-fry until the onion is tender. Add tomato purée, broccoli, dried oregano, salt and pepper. Reduce heat and simmer for 10 minutes or until broccoli is just tender. Add mushrooms and continue to heat for 5 minutes. Set this pizza sauce aside.

- Soak tempeh in soy sauce until most of the soy sauce is absorbed. Drain tempeh.

- Heat oil in a saucepan and fry tempeh , turning often, until golden brown. Add to pizza sauce and mix well.

- Spread sauce over each pita bread. Add chopped tomatoes and serve immediately.

NOTE

Alternatively, bake the pizzas in the oven at 180°C (350°F) for 5 minutes to give it an attractive brown crust before serving.

soy bean
sprout salad

Soy bean sprouts have a coarser texture and stronger taste than other bean sprouts. They go well with olive oil and sesame oil as shown in this recipe.

Serves 4

Ingredients

Soy bean sprouts	300 g (10½ oz), tailed and rinsed

Dressing

Sesame oil	½ Tbsp
Olive oil	½ Tbsp
White sesame seeds	1 Tbsp, crushed
Light soy sauce	2 Tbsp
Garlic	1 clove, peeled and crushed
Spring onions (scallions)	2, finely chopped
Honey or sugar	1 tsp
Cayenne pepper	¼ tsp or to taste

Method

- Bring a large pot of water to the boil and blanch soy bean sprouts for 1 minute. Drain well, then plunge into a basin of cold water immediately. Drain and set aside

- Combine all ingredients for the dressing.

- Toss sprouts gently in dressing. Chill before serving.

bean curd skin & soy noodles

deep-fried bean curd skin with spring onions

Bean curd skin is commonly fried on its own or used as a wrapper for meat or vegetables in Chinese cooking and the results are extremely tasty!

Serves 4

Ingredients

Dried bean curd skin	16 sheets, each 20 x 20-cm (8 x 8-in)
Eggs	3
Spring onions (scallions)	4, minced
Chinese five-spice powder	1 tsp
Salt	½ tsp
Light soy sauce	1 Tbsp

Method

- Wipe bean curd skins with a wet tea towel and gently pat dry, being careful not to tear them.

- Break eggs into a bowl and add spring onions, five-spice powder, salt and soy sauce. Beat well to mix.

- Lay 1 sheet of bean curd skin on a flat work surface and brush with beaten egg mixture. Place another sheet of bean curd skin on top, then fold into quarters. Repeat to brush and fold remaining bean curd skins.

- Cut folded bean curd skins into triangles.

- Heat oil for deep-frying, then lower bean curd triangles in to cook for 5 minutes. Remove with a slotted spoon and drain well. Serve hot.

deep-fried bean curd skin rolls with prawn and corn

These seafood rolls can be served as part of a meal or as finger food.

Serves 4–6

Ingredients

Dried bean curd skin — 4 sheets, each 20 x 20-cm (8 x 8-in)

Shelled prawns (shrimps) — 250 g (9 oz)

Salt — 1/2 tsp

Ground white pepper — 1/4 tsp

Corn flour (cornstarch) — 1/2 Tbsp

Egg — 1, beaten

Corn kernels — 100 g (3 1/2 oz)

Cooking oil for deep-frying

To Seal

Plain (all-purpose) flour — 1 Tbsp

Water — 1 Tbsp

Method

- Wipe bean curd skins with a wet tea towel and pat dry, being careful not to tear them.

- Mince prawns, then season with salt, pepper, corn flour and egg. Place into a blender (food processor) with corn kernels and purée. Divide into 4 portions.

- Combine flour and water into a paste. This will be used to seal the bean curd skin rolls.

- Lay a bean curd sheet on a flat work surface, with one corner towards you. Spoon 1 portion of prawn purée in a horizontal line in the middle of skin. Fold the corner of bean curd skin nearest you over filling. Next, fold the left and right corners in. Roll to form a neat roll. Seal with water and flour mixture. Repeat to make 4 rolls.

- Heat oil for deep-frying. Lower bean curd rolls into hot oil and deep-fry until golden brown. Drain well on absorbent paper and serve.

deep-fried bean curd skin rolls with minced pork

This dish uses dried bean curd skin which, when wrapped and fried, is very crispy and tasty. You can substitute the pork with chicken or fish. A popular dish in Asia.

Serves 4–6

Ingredients

Minced pork	400 g (14 $\frac{1}{3}$ oz)
Water chestnuts	4, peeled and finely chopped
Dried prawns (shrimps)	1 Tbsp, soaked in warm water for 20 minutes
Dried Chinese mushrooms	4, soaked in warm water for 20 minutes
Dried bean curd skin	16 sheets, each 10 x 10-cm (4 x 4-in)
Cooking oil	4 Tbsp
Vegetable stock	180 ml (6 fl oz / $\frac{3}{4}$ cup)
Ginger	5-cm (2-in) knob, peeled and grated

Marinade

Chinese cooking wine	1 Tbsp
Salt	1 tsp
Ground white pepper	$\frac{1}{2}$ tsp

Seasoning

Salt	$\frac{1}{2}$ tsp
Light soy sauce	1 Tbsp
Ground white pepper	$\frac{1}{2}$ tsp

To Seal

Plain (all-purpose) flour	2 Tbsp
Water	2 Tbsp

Method

- Wipe bean curd skins with wet tea towel and gently pat dry, being careful not to tear them.

- Place pork in a bowl with marinade and mix well. Leave to marinate for 10 minutes.

- Drain dried prawns and chop finely. Drain mushrooms, remove and discard stems. Cut caps into small cubes. Add prawns and mushrooms to pork and mix until a paste is formed. Divide into 16 portions.

- Combine flour and water into a paste. This will be used to seal bean curd skin rolls.

- Lay a bean curd sheet on a flat work surface, with one corner towards you. Spoon 1 portion of pork paste in a horizontal line in the middle of skin. Fold the corner of the bean curd skin nearest to you over filling. Next, fold the left and right corners in. Roll to form a neat roll. Seal with water and flour mixture. Repeat to make 16 rolls.

- Heat oil in a wok and add bean curd rolls. Cook for 3 minutes. Add stock, seasoning and grated ginger. Simmer for 15 minutes.

- Remove rolls with a slotted spoon and arrange on a serving plate. Spoon sauce over and serve hot

chicken parcel

Wrapping the minced chicken in bean curd skin locks in the juices, creating a wonderfully fragrant and succulent dish.

Serves 4

Ingredients

Minced chicken breast	300 g (10½ oz)
Spring onions (scallions)	1, chopped finely
Ginger	2.5-cm (1-in) knob peeled and finely chopped
Egg	1, lightly beaten
Salt	½ tsp
Ground white pepper	¼ tsp
Chinese cooking wine (*hua tiao*)	3 tsp
Dried bean curd skin	1 large sheet
Egg whites	4
Corn flour (cornstarch)	1 Tbsp
Cooking oil for deep-frying	

Method

- Wipe bean curd skins with wet tea towel and gently pat dry, being careful not to tear them.
- Combine minced chicken with spring onion, ginger, half the egg, salt, pepper and cooking wine.
- Brush remaining egg over bean curd skin and spoon minced chicken onto the centre. Bring edges of bean curd skin up to enclose filling and fold into a neat rectangular parcel. Trim off any excess skin. Flatten parcel by placing a chopping board on it.
- Place parcel in a steamer and steam for 15 minutes over high heat. Remove and leave to cool.
- Beat egg whites until light and fluffy. Stir in corn flour to make a thick paste. Brush over steamed parcel.
- Heat oil and deep-fry parcel until golden. Drain well and slice to serve.

deep-fried bean curd skin rolls

This vegetarian dish is often served in Chinese or vegetarian restaurants. It works well as a snack or as an appetiser.

Serves 4

Ingredients

Dried bean curd skin	3 sheets
Water	85 ml (2$\frac{1}{2}$ fl oz / $\frac{1}{3}$ cup)
Vegetable stock cube	$\frac{1}{4}$
Light soy sauce	1$\frac{1}{2}$ Tbsp
Sugar	1 tsp
Sesame oil	2 tsp
Cooking oil for deep-frying	
Kitchen string	
Cheesecloth	1, large sheet

Method

- Wipe bean curd skins with a wet tea towel, being careful not to tear them. Cut each sheet in half to get 6 sheets.

- Place water, stock cube, soy sauce, sugar and sesame oil in a small saucepan and heat, stirring, until stock cube and sugar dissolve. Remove from heat and leave to cool slightly.

- Lay cheesecloth on a flat work surface and place 1 sheet of bean curd skin on it. Brush with warm soy sauce mixture, then layer with another sheet of bean curd skin. Repeat to brush and layer until ingredients are used up.

- Roll bean curd sheets up tightly to form a cylinder and wrap with cheesecloth. Tie ends with kitchen string to keep roll in shape.

- Place roll in a steamer and steam, covered, over high heat for 10–12 minutes.

- Remove steamed roll carefully from steamer and remove cheesecloth. Cut roll into 4 rounds.

- Heat oil over high heat and deep-fry rolls until golden brown. Be careful, as it will splatter. Drain well. Slice into smaller pieces and serve hot or cold.

sweet bean curd skin dessert

This Chinese dessert is light and refreshing and can be served both hot or cold. It is known as fu chok tong shui in Cantonese.

Serves 4

Ingredients

Bean curd sticks	180 g (6$\frac{1}{3}$ oz), soaked until soft and drained
Canned gingko nuts	30
Rock sugar	125 g (4$\frac{1}{2}$ oz)
Water	1 litre (32 fl oz / 4 cups)
Eggs	2, lightly beaten

Method

- Break bean curd sticks into shorter lengths and place into a pot. Add all other ingredients except eggs.
- Bring mixture to the boil, then reduce heat and simmer for about 1 hour 30 minutes until bean curd sticks are very soft and broken up.
- Remove from heat and pour egg into soup in a steady stream, from about 10-cm (4-in) above pot, while stirring in one direction, to form thin ribbons.
- Serve hot or refrigerate and serve cold.

noodle salad with spicy dressing

This salad uses soy noodles as a main ingredient and comes with a spicy dressing. Omit the red chilli if a less spicy dish is preferred.

Serves 4

Ingredients

Soy noodles	250 g (9 oz)
Soy bean sprouts	140 g (5 oz)
Cherry tomatoes	2, sliced
Spring onions (scallions)	5, finely chopped
Baby corn	110 g (4 oz), chopped into bite-size pieces
Snow peas	140 g (5 oz), blanched
Coriander leaves (cilantro)	140 g (5 oz), chopped
Prawns (shrimps)	10, medium, peeled, deveined and cooked

Dressing

Thai basil leaves	250 g (9 oz)
Peanuts	60 g (2 oz), roasted
Olive oil	1 Tbsp
Sesame oil	1 tsp
Fish sauce	2 Tbsp
Light soy sauce	5 Tbsp
Fresh red chilli	1, seeded
Chilli sauce	1 tsp
Brown sugar	1 tsp

Dressing

Lime juice	4 Tbsp
Garlic	3 cloves, peeled

Garnish

Fresh basil and chopped peanuts (to taste)

Method

- Place noodles in a pot of boiling water. After 1–3 minutes, turn off heat and cover the pot, allowing the noodles to soften in the hot water for 10–15 minutes.

- Meanwhile, place dressing ingredients in a blender (food processor) and blend into a paste. Set aside.

- Taste the noodles to make sure they are soft enough to eat. Drain noodles and transfer to a large mixing bowl. Add soy bean sprouts while noodles are still hot and gently toss to cook the soy bean sprouts lightly.

- Add cherry tomatoes, spring onions, baby corn, snow peas, coriander and cooked prawns. Toss to mix, then add dressing and toss again.

- Add more fish sauce or soy sauce to taste if necessary.

- Place on a serving platter or in a salad dish and garnish as desired. Serve immediately.

fried noodles with mixed vegetables

This light noodle dish can be served on its own or with other stir-fried vegetable and meat dishes for a more substantial meal.

Serves 4

Ingredients

Cooking oil	2 Tbsp
Shallots (onions)	6 peeled and finely chopped
Garlic	4 cloves, peeled and finely chopped
Chinese cabbage	6 leaves, washed and cut into strips
Carrot	1, peeled and sliced
Soy noodles	500 g (18 oz), cooked in boiling water till soft and drained
Bean sprouts (mung beans)	300 g (10½ oz), tailed and rinsed

Seasoning

Water	250 ml (8 fl oz / 1 cup)
Oyster sauce	2 Tbsp
Light soy sauce	2 Tbsp
Sugar	1 tsp
Ground white pepper	½ tsp
Salt	¼ tsp

Garnish

Eggs	3, made into an omelette and shredded
Coriander leaves (cilantro)	

Method

- Heat oil in wok and fry shallots and garlic until lightly brown.
- Add cabbage and carrot, then stir-fry lightly for 1–2 minutes.
- Add soy noodles and toss well.
- Combine seasoning ingredients and pour into wok. Cover and leave for 10 minutes.
- Remove cover and add bean sprouts. Toss to mix then remove from wok.
- Serve garnished with omelette and coriander.

soy noodles with herb butter

The soy noodles, together with vegetables and cheese make a nutritious meal containing protein, fibre and vitamin B.

Serves 4.

Ingredients

Baby carrots	100 g (3½ oz)
Baby corn	100 g (3½ oz)
French beans	100 g (3½ oz)
Red capsicum (bell pepper)	1, seeded and cut into thin, long strips
Salt	½ tsp
Soy noodles	350 g (12½ oz), cooked in boiling water until soft and drained
Herb butter	55 g (2 oz)
Feta cheese	100 g (3½ oz), crumbled

Method

- Cut carrots, corn and French beans into lengths of 3.5-cm (1½-in).
- Bring a pot of water to the boil and add salt. Simmer vegetables for 5–8 minutes or until tender and then drain.
- Place soy noodles in a mixing bowl. Add vegetables and herb butter, then toss well.
- Transfer to a salad dish. Top with crumbled feta cheese and serve immediately.

soy milk
& soy flour

creamy tomato soup

This creamy soup can also be prepared with canned tomatoes for an even stronger tomato flavour.

Serves 4

Ingredients

Silken bean curd	300 g (10½ oz)
Cooking oil	½ Tbsp
Onion	1, peeled and minced
Garlic	1 clove, peeled and minced
Tomato	1, peeled and diced
Basil	2–3 leaves
Unsweetened soy milk (use store-bought or see p 66)	250 ml (8 fl oz / 1 cup)
Salt	to taste
Ground white pepper	to taste

Method

- Wrap silken bean curd in a clean tea towel and place on a plate. Place another plate on it to weigh it down. Refrigerate for 30 minutes to remove excess moisture. When bean curd is ready, remove from refrigerator and mash. Set aside.

- Heat oil in a saucepan. Cook onion and garlic over low heat until soft and onion looks transparent. Add tomato, basil and soy milk, stirring constantly, for 2 minutes.

- Remove from heat and pour contents of saucepan into a blender (food processor). Add mashed bean curd and purée until smooth.

- Return mixture to saucepan and cook over low heat, stirring constantly, until soup is warm. Season to taste with salt and pepper. Garnish as desired and serve immediately.

soy milk jelly

This tasty and nutritious jelly is an attractive dessert that can be served as part of a buffet or party spread.

Ingredients

Mango Jelly Layer

Ripe mango	1, large
Agar-agar powder	1 tsp
Water	125 ml (4 fl oz / $^1/_2$ cup)

Soy Milk Panna Cotta

Agar-agar powder	2 tsp
Sweetened soy milk (use store-bought or see p 66)	400 ml (13$^1/_2$ fl oz / 1$^1/_2$ cups)
Sugar or honey	to taste

Method

- Prepare mango layer. Peel and slice mango, then blend (process) flesh to get $^1/_2$ cup of purée.
- Combine agar-agar powder and water in a saucepan over low heat, stirring to dissolve agar-agar. When agar-agar is dissolved, add mango pulp and bring to the boil, stirring constantly.
- Pour mango jelly into individual serving moulds and leave to cool. Mango jelly should fill only one-third of each mould. Refrigerate until lightly set.
- Prepare panna cotta. Combine agar-agar powder and soy milk in a saucepan over low heat, stirring to mix well. When agar-agar is completely dissolved, stir in sugar or honey to taste. Bring mixture to the boil and remove from heat.
- Pour mixture equally into moulds over lightly set mango jelly. Leave to cool before refrigerating until set. Serve cold.

tropical smoothie

This blended beverage has a rich and thick consistency, resembling a milkshake but it is non-dairy.

Serves 4

Ingredients

Silken bean curd	55 g (2 oz)
Sweetened soy milk (use store-bought or see p 66)	180 ml (6 fl oz / $^3/_4$ cup)
Ripe mango	$^1/_2$ peeled and seeded
Ripe papaya	$^1/_2$ peeled and seeded
Ripe banana	1, medium
Freshly squeezed orange juice	60 ml (2 fl oz / $^1/_4$ cup)
Honey	to taste

Method

- Refrigerate all ingredients except banana until sufficiently chilled.
- Peel and cut banana into smaller pieces. Combine all ingredients in a blender (food processor) and blend until smooth. Pour into glasses and serve immediately.

pina colada smoothie

This smoothie is inspired by the rum-based cocktail, but does not contain rum.

Serves 4

Ingredients

Ripe banana	1, medium, peeled
Coconut milk	3 Tbsp
Unsweetened soy milk (use store-bought or see p 66)	435 ml (14 fl oz / $1^3/_4$ cups)
Unsweetened pineapple juice	500 ml (16 fl oz / 2 cups)
Honey	2 Tbsp

Method

- Refrigerate all ingredients except banana until sufficiently chilled.
- Peel and cut banana into smaller pieces. Combine all ingredients in a blender (food processor) and blend until smooth.
- Pour into glasses and serve immediately.

soy peanut cookies

The soy flour gives these cookies a light and moist texture, and an inviting soy flavour.

Makes 45–50 small cookies

Ingredients

Shelled peanuts	120 g (4$^1/_3$ oz), roasted, with skins removed
Castor (superfine) sugar	140 g (5 oz)
Vanilla essence	1 tsp
Soy flour	55 g (2 oz)
Plain (all-purpose) flour	125 g (4$^1/_2$ oz)
Vegetable oil	125 ml (4 fl oz / $^1/_2$ cup)

Method

- Grind peanuts in a blender (food processor) until very fine.

- Pour ground peanuts into a mixing bowl and add sugar, vanilla and both flours. Mix well, then make a well in the centre and pour in oil. Combine into a crumbly dough.

- Pinch a small amount of dough and shape into a firm ball about 2.5-cm (1-in) in diameter. Press dough ball lightly to flatten and place on a greased baking tray.

- Bake cookies in a preheated oven at 180°C (350°F) for 20 minutes or until lightly brown. Remove cookies and place on a wire rack to cool before serving or storing in an airtight container.

soy oat cookies

These cookies are great for a tea party or as a snack. Store in an airtight container for up to 1 week.

Makes 24–30 cookies

Ingredients

Soft margarine	70 g (2$\frac{1}{2}$ oz)
Vegetable oil	125 ml (4 fl oz / $\frac{1}{2}$ cup)
Castor (superfine) sugar	85 g (3 oz)
Egg	1, beaten
Vanilla essence	$\frac{1}{2}$ tsp
Soy flour	55 g (2 oz)
Self-raising flour	120 g (4$\frac{1}{2}$ oz)
Salt	$\frac{1}{2}$ tsp
Oats	2 Tbsp

Method

- Cream the margarine and vegetable oil together in a mixing bowl, then beat in sugar until light and fluffy. Fold in half of the beaten egg and vanilla essence.

- Sift in flours and salt. Mix lightly to form a soft dough.

- Divide the dough into 24 small pieces. Shape each piece into a ball about 2.5-cm (1-in) in diameter. Coat each ball in oats, then place on a greased baking tray. Press dough balls lightly to flatten.

- Bake cookies in a preheated oven at 180°C (350°F) for 15 minutes or until golden brown. Remove cookies and place on a wire rack to cool before serving or storing in an airtight container.

pancakes with grated coconut filling

These soy pancakes have a slightly nutty flavour compared to regular wheat flour pancakes.

Serves 4

Ingredients

Cooking oil
  for frying

Pancakes

Egg	1, beaten
Salt	½ tsp
Soy flour	55 g (2 oz)
Sweetened soy milk (use store-bought or see p 66)	150 ml (5 fl oz) + more if necessary

Coconut Filling

Brown sugar	55 g (2 oz)
Water	125 ml (4 fl oz / ½ cup)
Grated coconut	200 g (7 oz)
Vanilla essence	½ tsp

Method

- Prepare pancake batter. Combine all pancake ingredients in a bowl and stir until smooth. The batter should resemble the consistency of unwhipped double (heavy) cream. Add more soy milk if necessary. Cover and set aside.

- For the filling, heat sugar and water in a saucepan. Stir constantly, until sugar is dissolved. Add coconut and vanilla, then simmer, stirring constantly, until liquid is absorbed and coconut is just moist. Set aside.

- Lightly grease a frying pan over medium heat. Pour a small ladleful of batter into pan and tilt the pan around so batter coats the base of the pan. Cook until underside of pancake is lightly brown, then flip it over to cook the other side. Transfer pancake to a warmed oiled plate and cover with greaseproof paper to separate the pancakes. Repeat until ingredients are used up.

- Spoon some coconut filling onto each pancake and fold in half. Serve warm or at room temperature.

banana soy muffins

These delicious muffins do not contain eggs, making them perfect for those who are allergic to eggs.

Makes 6 large or 12 small muffins

Ingredients

Self-raising flour	480 g (17 oz)
Salt	1 tsp
Baking powder	2 Tbsp
Ripe bananas	4, large
Vegetable oil	170 ml (5$\frac{2}{3}$ fl oz)
Honey	8 Tbsp
Sweetened soy milk (use store-bought or see p 66)	250 ml (8 fl oz / 1 cup)

Method

- Preheat oven to 180°C (350°F). Line a 6-hole or 12-hole muffin tin with paper cups.
- Place flour in a large mixing bowl and sift salt and baking powder into bowl. Mix well and set aside.
- Peel and mash bananas, then mix well with oil, honey and soy milk.
- Gradually fold flour into banana mixture until just combined.
- Pour batter into lined muffin tin and bake for 30 minutes until tops are golden brown. Remove from oven and leave to cool before serving.

double chocolate walnut soy muffins

Walnuts add extra crunch to these great-tasting chocolate muffins!
Makes 12 muffins

Ingredients

Cake flour	240 g (8½ oz)
Salt	½ tsp
Baking powder	1 Tbsp
Dark chocolate	85 g (3 oz), chopped
Milk chocolate	85 g (3 oz), chopped
Walnuts	100 g (3½ oz), chopped
Vegetable oil	85 ml (2½ fl oz / ⅓ cup)
Honey	4 Tbsp
Unsweetened soy milk (use store-bought or see p 66)	125 ml (4 fl oz / ½ cup)
Lemon	½, juice extracted

Method

- Preheat oven to 180°C (350°F). Line a 12-hole muffin tin with paper cups.
- Sift flour, salt and baking powder into a large mixing bowl. Add chopped chocolate and walnuts and mix well.
- In a separate bowl, combine oil, honey and soy milk. Gradually fold in flour mixture until just combined.
- Pour batter into lined muffin tin and bake for 30 minutes until tops are golden brown. Remove from oven and leave to cool before serving

fruit cake

This tasty vegan fruit cake is light and moist, and is great for those who are allergic to eggs.

Ingredients

Margarine	100 g (3½ oz)
Castor (superfine) sugar	150 g (5⅓ oz)
Self-raising flour	400 g (14⅓ oz)
Mixed spices	2 tsp
Dried mixed fruit	200 g (7 oz)
Unsweetened soy milk (use store-bought or see p 66)	180 ml (6 fl oz / ¾ cups)
Apple juice	125 ml (4 fl oz / ½ cup)

Method

- In a large mixing bowl, beat margarine and sugar till fluffy.
- Fold flour and mixed spices into mixture. Gradually add in dried mixed fruit.
- Mix soy milk and apple juice into batter. Do not over-mix.
- Pour batter into a round 20-cm (8-in) baking tin or a loaf tin. Bake in preheated oven at 180°C (350°F) for 25 minutes. Remove from oven and leave to cool before serving.

soy waffles

This all-time breakfast favourite is made with soy flour and soy milk. Cook as you would pancakes if you do not have a waffle maker.

Makes 8 waffles

Ingredients

Eggs	2, beaten
Sugar	2 tsp
Sweetened soy milk (use store-bought or see p 66)	375 ml (12 fl oz / 1½ cups)
Melted butter	2 tsp
Soy flour	60 g (2 oz)
Plain (all-purpose) flour	200 g (7 oz)
Salt	½ tsp
Baking powder	2 tsp
Ground cinnamon	1 tsp
Golden syrup, honey or jam	

Method

- In a mixing bowl, beat eggs with sugar until sugar melts.
- Stir in soy milk and melted butter.
- Place flours in another mixing bowl and sift in salt and baking powder.
- Gradually fold flours into egg mixture and sprinkle in ground cinnamon.
- Spoon some batter into a heated waffle maker and bake until golden brown. Repeat until ingredients are used up.
- Serve hot with golden syrup, honey or jam.

soy sponge cake

This soft and fluffy sponge cake is great as a teatime snack. Serve on its own or with a chocolate or fruit sauce if desired.

Makes 6–8 small cakes

Ingredients

Plain (all-purpose) flour	85 g (3$\frac{1}{2}$ oz)
Soy flour	55 g (2 oz)
Baking powder	$\frac{2}{3}$ tsp
Eggs	5
Castor (superfine) sugar	140 g (5 oz)
Water	80 ml (2$\frac{1}{2}$ fl oz / $\frac{1}{3}$ cup)
Vanilla essence	1 tsp
Melted butter	70 g (2$\frac{1}{2}$ oz)

Method

- Sift flours and baking powder into a mixing bowl.
- Beat eggs and sugar in another mixing bowl until light and fluffy. Then add water and vanilla essence to egg mixture.
- Fold in flour mixture, then melted butter and blend well.
- Grease 6–8 small cake tins. Fill each tin with batter until three-quarters full.
- Bake in a preheated oven at 180°C (350°F) for 17 minutes or until cakes are cooked.
- Remove from oven and place on a wire rack to cool before serving.

baked potato pie

The combination of soy milk and egg white gives this pie a very smooth texture and a lovely soy fragrance.

Makes 2 pies

Ingredients

Capsicums (bell peppers)	3, medium, combination of red, yellow and green
Potatoes	450 g (1 lb), medium, boiled
Onion	1, large, peeled and finely chopped
Salt	1/4 tsp
Unsweetened soy milk (use store-bought or see p 66)	300 ml (10 fl oz / 1 1/4 cups)
Egg whites	3
Plain (all-purpose) flour	180 g (6 1/3 oz)
Baking powder	1 tsp

Method

- Cut capsicums in half. Remove seeds and cut into small cubes. Set aside.

- Dice boiled potatoes.

- Grease two circular pie dishes, each 15-cm (6-in) in diameter. Cover the base of each dish with potatoes, then with chopped onion, and capsicum cubes. Sprinkle with salt.

- In a large mixing bowl, blend soy milk and egg whites. Sift flour and baking powder in batches into mixture and fold in until smooth.

- Pour mixture into pie dishes and bake in a preheated oven at 200°C (400°F) for 30 minutes.

- Leave to cool slightly before serving.

glossary

1. Bean curd sticks

The skin that forms from boiling soy milk is usually made into sheets or sticks. The sticks (shown here) are hard and brittle. They are used in both sweet and savoury preparations.

2. Black bean paste

This Chinese black bean paste is made by fermenting black soy beans and flavouring it with spices. The salty paste is quite rich and is usually used in Asian stir-fries or for seasoning meat, poultry and vegetables.

3. Cayenne pepper

This generally refers to the powder, ground from the fiery fruit. A member of the capsicum family, cayenne pepper adds a spicy flavour to dishes. If unavailable, substitute with chilli powder which is similar in taste but coarser in texture.

4. Dried prawns (shrimps)

These dried prawns come in a variety of sizes and need to be soaked to soften before use. When fried, they give off a very strong flavour, and are used to season noodle, rice or vegetable dishes. They can also be used to flavour soups.

5. Feta cheese

This is a Greek curd cheese that comes soaked in brine. It has a sharp and salty taste and is traditionally made from the milk of sheep and goats. The texture is crumbly and is excellent in salads.

6. Flowering chives

This is one of several varieties of Chinese chives, used commonly for stir-fries, soups and salads. Flowering chives have a mild flavour and should only be lightly cooked.

7. Hoisin sauce
This thick reddish-brown sauce is made from fermented soy beans, spices and sugar. It is used widely in Chinese cooking to flavour meat, poultry or seafood dishes. Store in the refrigerator after opening.

8. Miso
A thick paste made from fermenting soy beans, then mixed with wheat, and barley or rice. There are many varieties of miso, the two most common being brown and white miso (shown here). Miso is used in Japanese cooking as a condiment and flavouring.

9. Sake
This Japanese rice wine can be used for cooking or be consumed on its own as an alcoholic beverage.

10. Shoyu
A Japanese soy sauce, this has a lighter flavour and is less salty than Chinese soy sauce. It is used as a seasoning for cooking or as a condiment at the table.

11. Wakame
This edible kelp is available dried or fresh and is often used in soups and salads. Store dried wakame in a sealed or airtight container, placed in a cool, dry place.

12. Water chestnuts
These small, round corms of an aquatic plant have crisp, juicy white flesh that can be consumed raw or cooked. They are highly perishable and must be kept refrigerated.

13. Yellow bean paste
Like black bean paste, this is also made from fermenting salted soy beans. This paste is comparatively sweeter and milder. It is used to flavour stir-fried, stewed and braised dishes.

Weights and Measures

Quantities for this book are given in Metric, Imperial and American (spoon and cup) measures. Standard spoon and cup measurements used are: 1 tsp = 5 ml, 1 Tbsp = 15 ml, 1 cup = 250 ml. All measures are level unless otherwise stated.

Liquid And Volume Measures

Metric	Imperial	American
5 ml	1/6 fl oz	1 teaspoon
10 ml	1/3 fl oz	1 dessertspoon
15 ml	1/2 fl oz	1 tablespoon
60 ml	2 fl oz	1/4 cup (4 tablespoons)
85 ml	2 1/2 fl oz	1/3 cup
90 ml	3 fl oz	3/8 cup (6 tablespoons)
125 ml	4 fl oz	1/2 cup
180 ml	6 fl oz	3/4 cup
250 ml	8 fl oz	1 cup
300 ml	10 fl oz (1/2 pint)	1 1/4 cups
375 ml	12 fl oz	1 1/2 cups
435 ml	14 fl oz	1 3/4 cups
500 ml	16 fl oz	2 cups
625 ml	20 fl oz (1 pint)	2 1/2 cups
750 ml	24 fl oz (1 1/5 pints)	3 cups
1 litre	32 fl oz (1 3/5 pints)	4 cups
1.25 litres	40 fl oz (2 pints)	5 cups
1.5 litres	48 fl oz (2 2/5 pints)	6 cups
2.5 litres	80 fl oz (4 pints)	10 cups

Dry Measures

Metric	Imperial
30 grams	1 ounce
45 grams	1 1/2 ounces
55 grams	2 ounces
70 grams	2 1/2 ounces
85 grams	3 ounces
100 grams	3 1/2 ounces
110 grams	4 ounces
125 grams	4 1/2 ounces
140 grams	5 ounces
280 grams	10 ounces
450 grams	16 ounces (1 pound)
500 grams	1 pound, 1 1/2 ounces
700 grams	1 1/2 pounds
800 grams	1 3/4 pounds
1 kilogram	2 pounds, 3 ounces
1.5 kilograms	3 pounds, 4 1/2 ounces
2 kilograms	4 pounds, 6 ounces

Length

Metric	Imperial
0.5 cm	1/4 inch
1 cm	1/2 inch
1.5 cm	3/4 inch
2.5 cm	1 inch

Oven Temperature

	°C	°F	Gas Regulo
Very slow	120	250	1
Slow	150	300	2
Moderately slow	160	325	3
Moderate	180	350	4
Moderately hot	190/200	375/400	5/6
Hot	210/220	410/425	6/7
Very hot	230	450	8
Super hot	250/290	475/550	9/10

Abbreviation

tsp	teaspoon
Tbsp	tablespoon
g	gram
kg	kilogram
ml	millilitre